P9-CJH-109

101
uses
for a
LAB

101
uses
for a
LAB

PHOTOGRAPHY BY DALE C. SPARTAS

WILLOW CREEK PRESS
MINOCQUA, WISCONSIN

© 1998 Willow Creek Press
Photography © Dale C. Spartas

Published by Willow Creek Press
P.O. Box 147 • Minocqua, Wisconsin 54548

Design: Heather M. McElwain

For information on other Willow Creek titles,
call 1-800-850-9453

Individual custom prints of the photographs in this book are available directly from the photographer. Write to: Dale C. Spartas, P.O.Box 1367, Bozeman, MT 59771-1367; or call (406) 585–2244.

Library of Congress Cataloging-in-Publication Data

Spartas, Dale C.
   101 uses for a lab / photography by Dale C. Spartas.
   p.   cm.
   ISBN 1-57223-131-9
   1. Labrador retriever--Pictorial works. 2. Labrador retriever--Humor. I. Title.
   SF429.L3S56   1998
   636.752'7–dc21   98-10114
                                            CIP

Excerpts from *Desiderata* (© 1927 by Max Ehrmann. All rights reserved) appear throughout the chapter "Lab as Guru." Copyright renewed 1954 by Bertha K. Ehrmann. Reprinted by permission, Robert L. Bell, Melrose, MA 02176.

Printed in Canada

*Dedicated to the Labs,
the people who love them
and those who preserve
the integrity of the breed.*

— Dale C. Spartas

LABS
In and Around the House

Uses 1-22

1

*H*ouse security alarm

2

*B*order patrol

3

*A*larm clock

101 USES FOR A LAB

4

*C*lean pots and pans

5

Dishwasher

6

*G*arbage disposal

7

*C*ar wash

101 Uses for a Lab

*H*and towel and wash cloth

Q-tip

101 USES FOR A LAB

*P*illow

*S*omeone to antique your antiques

13

14

*B*reak in your shoes and garment alterations

15

*F*ield hand

101 USES FOR A LAB

*P*aper boy

17

*W*eed killer

101 Uses for a Lab

18

*L*awn sprinkler

*E*dge trimmer

101 Uses for a Lab

*G*ather firewood

*A*u pair

101 Uses for a Lab

22

*B*ook ends

Special Uses for LABS

Uses 23-57

*H*ugs on demand

101 USES FOR A LAB

*S*omeone to stick by you when others may not

31

*F*ishing *companion*

101 USES FOR A LAB

*H*unting companion

*A*ccomplice

Comedian

*T*o win friends

101 Uses for a Lab

. . . and influence people

*S*omeone to dress up with

32

. . . and to be seen with

33

*S*omeone to help pick up girls

101 Uses for a Lab

. . . or guys

*S*omeone to party with . . . and recuperate with

A gift

38

Manicurist

101 USES FOR A LAB

39

*H*and warmer

40

*S*addle pal

*A*rchaeologist

42

*C*o-pilot

*N*avigator

44

*F*irst mate

45

*B*ackseat driver

46

*H*ead waiter

101 Uses for a Lab

*T*aste tester

*D*rug sniffer

101 Uses for a Lab

49

*U*nderwater salvage

_50_

Guard the truck

*G*uard the car

*S*omeone to go places you wouldn't go yourself

*T*rail blazer

54

*S*omeone to grow up with

101 Uses for a Lab

55

Someone to grow old with

*B*est friend now

. . . and forever

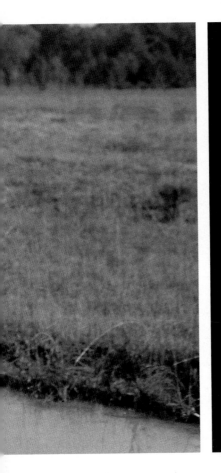

LABS
As Athletes

Uses 58-81

58

*T*o catch

. . . and retrieve a frisbee

*T*o retrieve dummies

101 Uses for a Lab

. . . toys

. . . sticks

101 Uses for a Lab

. . . kongs

64

. . . *shoes*

101 Uses for a Lab

. . . grooming accessories

. . . decoys

. . . duck dinner

. . . pheasant dinner

101 Uses for a Lab

. . . goose dinner

LABS AS ATHLETES

. . . grouse dinner

101 Uses for a Lab

. . . and a cold one

*S*ynchronized swimming

101 USES FOR A LAB

*O*lympic hurdler

74

*S*omeone to work out with

75

Soccer MVP

76

*T*o walk with

. . . to jog with

. . . to run with

. . . to hike with

. . . to compete with

. . . and to motivate you

LAB
As Guru

The Teachings of
Spiritual Advisor
Labba Ram Das

Uses 82-101

LABBA RAM DAS SAYS:

*"Go placidly amid the noise and haste
and remember what peace there may be in silence."*

"*Listen to others, even the dull and the ignorant;
they too have their story.*"

"Enjoy your friendships . . .

. . . but don't allow yourself to be taken advantage of."

86

"Be tolerant of others . . .

101 Uses for a Lab

. . . but only to a point."

"If you compare yourself to others
you may become vain and bitter, for always there will be
greater and lesser persons than yourself."

101 Uses for a Lab

"But, on the other hand, it's not bragging if you can do it."

90

"*Follow your instincts . . .*

101 Uses for a Lab

. . . and pursue your tasks with determination."

92

*"Remember, sharing is a virtue . . .
selfishness a sin."*

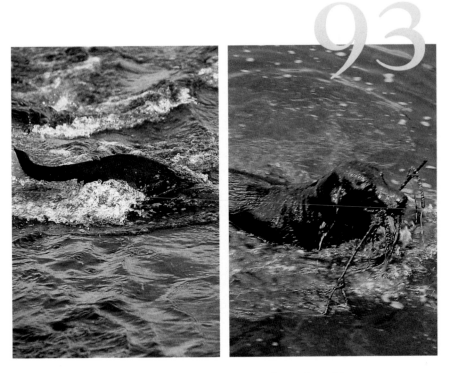

"Stay focused on the task at hand."

"Be of good humor and share your joy with others."

*"Exercise caution in your affairs,
for the world is full of trickery."*

"But let this not blind you to what virtue there is;

for everywhere life is full of heroism."

97

"Be yourself, especially do not feign affection."

*"Take kindly the counsel of the years
gracefully surrendering the things of youth."*

99

"Neither be cynical about love;
it is as perennial as the grass."

101 Uses for a Lab

"Keep peace with your soul. With all its shams, drudgery and broken dreams, it is still a beautiful world. Be cheerful. Strive to be happy."

"*You are a child of the universe,
no less than the trees and the stars:
you have a right to be here.*"